Presented to

_____

By

_____

Date

_____

BREATH PRAYERS

for *Women*

Simple Whispers That Keep You in God's Presence

HONOR **HB** BOOKS

Inspiration and Motivation for the Seasons of Life

imprint of Cook Communications Ministries • Colorado Springs, CO

Unless otherwise indicated, all Scripture quotations are taken from the *Holy Bible, New International Version*®. NIV ®. Copyright © 1973, 1978, 1984 by International Bible Society. Used by permission of Zondervan Publishing House. All rights reserved.

Scripture quotations marked KJV are taken from the *King James Version* of the Bible.

Scripture quotations marked NRSV are taken from the *New Revised Standard Version* of the Bible, copyright © 1989 by The Division of Christian Education of the National Council of the Churches of Christ in the USA. Used by permission. All rights reserved.

Scripture quotations marked AMP are taken from *The Amplified Bible, New Testament* copyright © 1958, 1987 by The Lockman Foundation, La Habra, California. Used by permission.

Scripture quotations marked TLB are taken from *The Living Bible* © 1986. © 1971. Used by permission of Tyndale House Publishers, Inc., Wheaton, Illinois 60189. All rights reserved.

Scripture quotations marked NLT are taken from the *Holy Bible, New Living Translation,* copyright © 1996. Used by permission of Tyndale House Publishers, Inc., Wheaton, Illinois 60189. All rights reserved.

Scripture quotations marked NKJV are taken from *The New King James Version.* Copyright © 1979, 1980, 1982, 1994, Thomas Nelson, Inc.

Scripture quotations marked NCV are taken from the *Holy Bible, New Century Version,* copyright © 1987, 1988, 1991, by Word Publishing, Dallas, Texas 75039. Used by permission.

08 07 06 05   10 9 8 7 6 5 4 3 2

Breath Prayers for Women—
Simple Whispers That Keep You in God's Presence
ISBN 1-56292-254-8

Copyright © 2004 Bordon Books
6532 East 71st Street, Suite 105
Tulsa, OK 74133

Published by Honor Books,
An Imprint of Cook Communications Ministries
4050 Lee Vance View
Colorado Springs, CO 80918

Developed by Bordon Books
Produced by Grasshopper Productions
Manuscript written by Betsy Williams of Williams Services, Inc.

WHAT IS A BREATH PRAYER?

Even if you spend time in the morning with God, by the time you've finished item number ten on your list of things to do, the peace you felt may have evaporated; and perhaps He feels very far away. But He is as close as your breath; and you can spend your entire day with Him—even on the run. Breath prayers are brief, heartfelt prayers that can help you to enjoy God's company and surround your loved ones with prayer without retreating to the mountains and giving up your to do list. The secret is a short prayer that you whisper to God as you go about the business of your day, allowing your experiences to prompt you. As you see a friend, you can pray, "Father, bless her." As you stand in line, you can prayer "Father, bless her" for the cashier as someone argues with her. When you get to that three o'clock slump and wonder how you are going to get everything done, you can pray, "Father, bless me."

Instead of leaving God in the corner with your Bible or other devotional books, breath prayers can help you to live a life in which God walks with you daily as you talk to Him about the things that cross your path. Your life will be transformed as you live continually in God's presence.

Best of all is it to preserve
everything in a pure, still heart,
and let there be for every
pulse a thanksgiving,
and for every breath a song.

KONRAD VON GESNER

Pray without ceasing.

1 THESSALONIANS 5:17 NKJV

How to Use
Breath Prayers for Women

After you have read *Breath Prayers for Women,* choose a suitable prayer to use throughout your day. Repeat it so that you can say it to yourself in one breath, both in and out. Each breath is a prayer. In this way you will pray without ceasing, aware of God walking through each experience with you.

As you see people or think of them, as you experience situations or feelings, offer that prayer to God. "I exalt You, Lord," can become the refrain of your heart when you see drivers around you on the road and as you see various people. "I exalt You, Lord," can mean you celebrate with God others' existence. It can mean you celebrate God's Lordship and loving care of them. It can also mean you praise God even though things are not going your way at the moment. The words will stay the same, but each breath you pray will be unique in the way you mean it to God. And you will maintain a constant connection with Him.

[Pray] always with all prayer and
supplication in the Spirit, being watchful
to this end with all perseverance
and supplication for all the saints.

EPHESIANS 6:18 NKJV

BE MY ROCK, LORD.

The LORD is my rock,
my fortress and my deliverer;
my God is my rock,
in whom I take refuge.

PSALM 18:2 NIV

There are times when you might feel like you are being swallowed up by quicksand. Your emotions are overwhelming, threatening to drag you under. Or perhaps things are changing so rapidly around you that you need something solid to grab onto.

Have you ever heard the phrase, "hard as a rock" or heard of a person referred to as "the rock of Gibraltar"? Well, God wants to be your rock. Tougher than the hardest diamond and unmoved by any circumstance, He stands firm and solid, Someone you can hold onto. Or if you just need to take a break and rest awhile, He is your rock of refuge, hiding you inside His strength from the storms of life.

I can pray the breath prayer, *Be my rock, Lord,* when—

- I need to stand strong.

- I am scared.

- the winds of change are blowing around me.

- I feel wishy-washy.

- I have failed.

- I need someone to hold onto.

- I need a break from my circumstances.

Be my rock, Lord.

KEEP ME SAFE, MOST HIGH.

If you make the Most High your dwelling—
even the LORD, who is my refuge—
then no harm will befall you,
no disaster will come near your tent.

PSALM 91:9-10 NIV

Are you afraid? Perhaps you are flying out of town on business, leaving your family behind. Maybe severe weather threatens your neighborhood, or you are caught out in a storm. Perhaps you fear being hurt by another person—either physically or emotionally. Or maybe your immediate circumstances are fine but you fear what *could* happen.

There is no place on Earth safer than in the shelter of God's protection. He is the ultimate hiding place, keeping you safe from harm. He's given His angels an assignment to watch over you, to guard you everywhere you go. When life gets scary and you feel full of fear, God is right there to protect you. He is your shield, and you can trust Him to keep you safe.

I can pray the breath prayer, *Keep me safe, Most High,* when—

- I fly on an airplane.

- inclement weather is headed my way.

- I am away from home.

- terrorists terrorize.

- the news is filled with scary reports.

- someone tries to hurt me.

Keep me safe, Most High.

YOU ARE MY HOPE, MY SAVIOR.

Why are you downcast, O my soul?
Why so disturbed within me?
Put your hope in God,
for I will yet praise him,
my Savior.

PSALM 42:5 NIV

Hopelessness. You can see it in the faces of so many people. Maybe you see it in your own face today as you look in the mirror. Perhaps you are facing a crisis, and all of the facts say that it's all over, so you might as well give up. Or you are facing a situation that has been going on for so long that you have become weary and no longer see any reason to be hopeful? Does there appear to be no way out? Have you lost all hope?

Well, if that describes you, here's the good news. There is *always* hope with God. Even when the circumstances say otherwise, you can hope against hope, because God can and does work miracles. Your situation may be beyond the help of man; but God is your hope, and He is working on your behalf.

I can pray the breath prayer, *You are my hope, my Savior,* when—

- I see no way out.

- no person can do anything to help.

- my emotions are spiraling downward.

- I can't do anything to change my situation.

- I need a miracle.

- all appears lost.

You are my hope, my Savior.

RESTORE MY HONOR.

*You will give me greater honor than before
and turn again and comfort me.*

PSALM 71:21 TLB

Scorned. Humiliated. Laughed at. Ridiculed.
Have you ever been in a situation where others
looked upon you with disdain? It could have
been the result of some failure on your part, the
color of your skin, or because you have been
abused. Or perhaps you have been falsely
accused of something. Any of these situations
would cause you to hang your head in shame.

But this is not the stature of a child of God.
This is not the end of your story. No situation is
beyond the help of God. He will cleanse you if
you need cleansing. He will restore your reputation. He honors you and places great value on
you because you are His child. He favors you

and surrounds you with favor as a shield.
Instead of being bowed down, stand up and hold
your head high. You are a child of the King!

I can pray the breath prayer, *Restore my honor,*
when—

- others look down on me.

- I am ashamed of myself.

- my reputation has been destroyed.

- I have failed You.

- I have been rejected.

Restore my honor.

HELP!

*In my distress I screamed to the Lord
for his help. And he heard me from heaven;
my cry reached his ears.*

PSALM 18:6 TLB

Are you in a crisis? Has panic gripped your heart? Do you need help *now*? You may never find yourself in a critical or life-and-death situation. But chances are, at some point you will encounter circumstances or you will find yourself requiring help that can't wait, help you need sooner than later, help you need *now*.

What a relief it is to know that Jesus is as close as the mention of His name! Unlike a flesh-and-blood person, He is always with you, and He will never leave you nor forsake you. He has promised to give you well-timed help in your hour of need. He may use another person to provide the aid, or He may give you the wisdom and understanding needed to resolve the situation. The bottom line is, He will give you what you need, when you need it. He is your help.

I can pray the breath prayer, *Help!,* when—

- tragedy strikes.

- I have hurt myself.

- my car has broken down on the side of the road.

- I am at the scene of an accident.

- I think I'm having a heart attack.

- something has happened to my child.

Help!

I WILL BE STILL
AND KNOW.

Be still, and know that I am God.

PSALM 46:10 NIV

Be still. *Sure,* you think as thoughts bombard your mind. Easier said than done when your to-do list is never-ending, there are phone calls to return, you log on to find fifty e-mails, and—if you have children—you're peppered with "Hey, Mommy!" till you want to change your name. Then there's noise—traffic, the phone ringing off the hook, roofers next door, an occasional siren, the TV blaring, the radio, the dog barking, the washing machine. You are surrounded with noise, confusion, turmoil, and action. Everything but stillness.

But there is a secret for those who know God

—a quiet place where only the two of you can go. At a moment's notice, He can take you into His secret chamber where you can *be still and know* that He is God—you are loved, you are safe, you are treasured, He will provide for you, He will never leave or forsake you. He is God.

I can pray the breath prayer, *I will be still and know,* when—

- my thoughts are anxious.

- I am afraid.

- I have too much to do.

- I am stressed out.

- life seems out of control.

- my mind is racing.

I will be still and know.

LET ME HEAR
YOUR VOICE.

*Whether you turn to the right
or to the left, your ears will hear
a voice behind you, saying,
"This is the way; walk in it."*

ISAIAH 30:21 NIV

What in the world am I supposed to do?
Perhaps you're asking yourself that right now. A
lot may be riding on your decision, too; and you
can't afford to make a mistake.

When you can't see the forest for the trees,
your heavenly Father sees the big picture from
on high and promises to tell you which road to
take. He may speak to you in the form of a prevailing thought, a scripture, or even the voice of
a friend. But He will tell you. As you take each

step, He will guide you by His peace to the next one. Step by step, He'll show you what to do.

I can pray the breath prayer, *Let Me hear Your voice,* when—

- I am perplexed by a situation.

- when I come to a crossroads and have to choose a path.

- my children rebel, and I need to know how to handle it.

- I have to make decisions regarding an ailing parent.

- I am in an abusive relationship.

- I see corruption in my workplace.

Let me hear Your voice.

MAY I LOOK WITH YOUR EYES OF LOVE, LORD.

The LORD does not look at the things man looks at. Man looks at the outward appearance, but the LORD looks at the heart.

1 SAMUEL 16:7 NIV

Don't judge a book by its cover. Most would agree that this is a wise principle to follow. But do we? Often we are not even aware of our snap assessments. Whether it is the color of another person's skin or the shiny paint job on a car we're thinking about buying, looks can be—and often are—deceiving.

This may be human nature, but thankfully it is not God's. He judges based on what is in the heart. None of us likes to be misjudged, nor do we want to be deceived by something beautiful on the outside, only to find that what is beneath the surface is rotten. By seeing through God's eyes, we can make sound decisions as well as offer the same gift of unconditional love to others that God extends to us.

I can pray the breath prayer, *May I look with Your eyes of love, Lord,* when—

- my perception is skewed.

- I meet someone for the first time.

- someone is hurtful toward me.

- I am judgmental.

- someone is different from me.

- people are hard to get along with.

May I look with Your eyes of love, Lord.

COMFORT ME, FATHER.

*As a mother comforts her child,
so will I comfort you;
and you will be comforted.*

ISAIAH 66:13 NIV

Are you in pain? Is it a chronic, dull ache?
A piercing agony that threatens to do you in?
Maybe someone you love has left—through
divorce, abandonment, or death. Perhaps you
have failed.

Did you know that pain is actually a good
thing? If you touch a hot stove, pain alerts you
to remove your hand before greater damage is
done. Emotional pain serves a similar purpose.
It is the signal that your injury needs attention.
It is your cue to run to the Source of all comfort

24

before the wound further injures your soul.

Jesus promised that He would not leave you comfortless. True to that promise, He has sent the Comforter to soothe your pain, to pour the oil of His presence into your wounds to heal them. There is no pain that He cannot ease, no valley so deep that He will not go. In your darkest moment, He is there—to comfort you and bring you through to the light on the other side.

I can pray the breath prayer, *Comfort me, Father,* when—

- my heart is broken.

- I am disappointed.

- I have been abandoned.

- someone I love dies.

- I grieve over something I have lost.

- when I have failed.

Comfort me, Father.

I WILL PRAISE YOU.

*My mouth is filled with your praise,
declaring your splendor all day long.*

PSALM 71:8 NIV

It's easy to praise God during good times,
but what about when life is in turmoil? It is then
that praise becomes an act of the will, a sacrifice,
and . . . a weapon.

A weapon? Consider the following examples.

God instructed Jehoshaphat to send the
praisers ahead of his army. As they praised God,
the Lord set ambushes against their enemies,
resulting in a great victory.

The Lord instructed the children of Israel to
walk around the walls of Jericho, blowing their
trumpets. Then, following their great shout, the
walls crumbled before them.

When in prison, instead of bemoaning their

26

circumstances, Paul and Silas sang praises at midnight. Suddenly, there was a great earthquake and the prison doors opened.

Are you in a midnight hour? Against all human reasoning, begin to lift your voice in praise to your Father. Your miracle is on its way. Praise Him all the way to the victory, and then continue to praise Him for His mighty acts.

I can pray the breath prayer, *I will praise You,* when—

- enemies surround me.

- I'm up against a brick wall.

- I'm in my midnight hour.

- my miracle comes.

- I recognize my love for You.

I will praise You.

MAKE ME A PEACEMAKER.

Blessed are *the peacemakers: for they shall be called the children of God.*

MATTHEW 5:9 KJV

Don't you get tired of all the hatred in the world? Everywhere you look, you can see evidence of it—nation warring against nation, ethnic cleansing, gang violence, lawsuits. Hatred is also evident closer to home—sibling rivalry, family strife, and divorce. People have a hard time getting along with others. One act of hatred seems to breed another and another.

You wonder how you can make a difference when you are only one person and you have no control over the choices others make. It's not your responsibility to reconcile the whole world, but what you can do is pray for peace. Learn healthy ways to resolve conflict, and work at making peace with those who are at odds with you. Extend your hand to your enemy. Turn the other cheek. Help others reconcile their differences. Point people to God.

God performed the ultimate peacemaking act when He reconciled the world to Himself through His Son, Jesus. You can be a peacemaker, too, because He lives in you.

I can pray the breath prayer, *Make me a peacemaker*—

- when there is strife in my family.

- when there seems to be an impasse at work.

- to mend broken relationships.

- when others wrong me.

- instead of a gossiper.

Make me a peacemaker.

MAKE ME A FRIEND LIKE YOU.

*"Greater love has no one than this,
that he lay down his life for his friends."*

JOHN 15:13 NIV

"Make new friends, but keep the old. One is silver; the other is gold." If you've ever had a good friend, you can vouch for the truth of this childhood song.

But maybe you are lacking in this area. Maybe a close friend has moved away or died. Maybe you are single and your best friend has just married. Maybe you have moved and are lonely. Or perhaps you have some relationships, but they're one-sided and unhealthy. Maybe you have just begun a walk with the Lord, and you need new friends who share your faith.

Whatever the case, know that friendships are God's idea, and you can count on Him to provide them. Keep in mind that in order to have good friends, you must be a good friend yourself. You can count on God to give you this desire of your heart, but remember, too, that Jesus is a friend who sticks closer than a brother, and He's the very best friend of all.

I can pray the breath prayer, *Make me a friend like You—*

- when I need friends.

- when I see someone standing alone.

- when others cross my path today.

- when I am tempted to reject others who are different.

- who will encourage others to grow.

Put a song in my heart, God.

I EMBRACE YOUR REST.

He makes me lie down in green pastures,
he leads me beside quiet waters,
he restores my soul.

PSALM 23:2-3 NIV

Stress has reached epidemic proportions in today's society. And even though cell phones, e-mail, and computers have made our lives more productive, the stress level has risen proportionately. Compromised immune systems, migraine headaches, sleep disturbances, and other stress-related ailments often warn us to take it easy, but it's usually more convenient to medicate the condition than to come a screeching halt.

God is not the author of stress. In fact, He rested on the seventh day of Creation and instructed man to follow suit. Hard work is both rewarding and fruitful, but when that work is done—and sometimes when it's not—the Good Shepherd invites you to follow Him to green pastures and quiet waters. When you take time for quiet reflection and to bask in His presence, you can then emerge energized, sharper in your mind, and with fresh enthusiasm to meet the world again.

I can pray the breath prayer, *I embrace Your rest,* when—

- I leave work.

- it's time to go to bed.

- I'm trying to meet a deadline.

- the stress level is off the Richter scale.

- it's time to rest.

- it's time to play.

I embrace Your rest.

MAY I SHARE YOUR ABUNDANCE.

God is able to provide you with every blessing in abundance, so that by always having enough of everything, you may share abundantly.

2 CORINTHIANS 9:8 NRSV

You know that God wants you to bless others, but did you know that He will provide the means by which you can? You can't give what you don't have, so He wants to bless you with abundance in order to meet the needs of others.

It is a spiritual principle that as you plant a seed of blessing, a harvest of blessing will return to you so you can give again. The more you give, the more you receive. The more you receive, the more you have to give; and so goes the cycle of

34

blessing that your generosity sets into motion.

Consider these ways to bless others: time spent listening, providing a meal, babysitting, a phone call, cleaning a home, washing a car, an encouraging word, running errands. Make it your great quest to be a blessing everywhere you go. You'll be the most blessed of all.

I can pray the breath prayer, *May I share Your abundance*—

- even when I am hurting, myself.

- to help me overcome selfishness.

- when others are hurting.

- so others will see Your goodness.

- so I can show others what You are like.

- to restore their hope.

May I share Your abundance.

HELP ME SEE
YOUR GOOD.

*In all things God works for the good
of those who love him, who have
been called according to his purpose.*

ROMANS 8:28 NIV

Do you tend to see the glass half empty or
half full? Recognizing the silver lining is a skill
any of us can develop. It's all about perspective.
Two people can share the same experience, yet
their perceptions can be altogether different.

First, you must know that God is good and
that He is only capable of doing good. The thief
is the one who steals, kills, and destroys; but
nothing he can throw at you is greater than God's
work on your behalf. God doesn't send trouble
your way, but He can and will turn situations

around for your good. Knowing this makes it easier to look for the good, even in the face of very negative circumstances.

As you go about your day today, consciously look for His goodness in every situation. It will be there. God will help you recognize it.

I can pray the breath prayer, *Help me see Your good*, when—

- tragedy strikes.

- things happen that I don't understand.

- I am disappointed.

- everything seems to be going wrong.

- all I can see is bad.

Help me see Your good.

SHOW ME YOUR WAYS.

*As the heavens are higher
than the earth, so are my ways
higher than your ways and
my thoughts than your thoughts.*

ISAIAH 55:9 NIV

So often, God's ways are the exact opposite of ours. The first chapter of 1 Corinthians describes the wisdom of God as being foolishness to those who don't know Him.

For example, human logic says that when you give, you forfeit what was once yours. God's way says that when you give, you receive—good measure, pressed down, shaken together, and running over. (See Luke 6:38.) Human logic reasons that "survival of the fittest" is the law of the land, and that to get to the top you have to climb over others. But Jesus said that many who are first shall be last, and the last shall be first. (See Mark 10:31.) Religion says that we have to earn salvation; God offers it as a free gift.

This is why it is so important to know God's Word and to learn to hear His voice. Living by human reason yields man's results. But doing things God's way produces results that are exceedingly, abundantly above all that we can ask or think. (See Ephesians 3:20.)

I can pray the breath prayer, *Show me Your ways,* in—

- obtaining professional success.

- dealing with others.

- resolving conflict.

- the financial arena.

- my family.

Show me Your ways.

ORDER MY STEPS, LORD.

Everything should be done in a fitting and orderly way.

1 CORINTHIANS 14:40 NIV

"A place for everything and everything in its place" sounds like a good idea doesn't it? It's quite aggravating to need the flashlight and not be able to find it as you stumble around in the dark.

Did you know that God is organized? In the book of Numbers, He instructs Moses to take a census, organize the twelve tribes, and appoint a leader over each. Jesus even organized the crowd before feeding the five thousand. (See Mark 6:39-44.)

Even if you are the most disorganized individual you know, there is always hope. If God can organize the universe, He can certainly help you bring order to your junk drawer. Start with something simple, like putting all those coupons into a card file organized by type of food or service. When you add new coupons, discard the expired ones. It seems like a small thing, but if you will ask God to help as you take small steps in different areas of your life, one by one they will lead to a more ordered and peaceful existence.

I can pray the breath prayer, *Order my steps, Lord—*

- in my financial affairs.

- in my home.

- at work.

- so that I can be more efficient.

- regarding my schedule.

Order my steps, Lord.

SHOW ME ALL TRUTH, SPIRIT OF TRUTH.

"When he, the Spirit of truth, comes, he will guide you into all truth."

JOHN 16:13 NIV

Have you ever discovered the truth about a matter after having been deceived? It can be devastating. Or, perhaps you have believed a lie that, when exposed, revealed tremendous blessing. For instance, say you had been guilt-ridden, believing you could never measure up to God's expectations. Then one day you read, "There is no condemnation for those who are in Christ Jesus" (Romans 8:1 NIV). That would be good news!

Jesus said that you would know the truth and the truth would set you free. (See John 8:32.)

At times the truth can be hard to swallow. But at other times, seeing the truth can change the course of history as it did when the zealous persecutor of Christians, Paul, ran right into the Truth on the road to Damascus.

Either way, the truth always leads to freedom, and the Holy Spirit is your personal guide to get you there.

I can pray the breath prayer, *Show me all truth, Spirit of Truth—*

- when I wonder who I am in Christ.

- when I am tempted to doubt.

- if I am deceived.

- when I need to know all the blessings Christ has provided for me.

- regarding anything that is askew in my family.

- even when I avoid it.

   Show me all truth, Spirit of Truth.

LET ME DREAM YOUR DREAMS, LORD.

The vision is yet for an appointed time;
But at the end it will speak, and it will not lie.
Though it tarries, wait for it;
Because it will surely come, It will not tarry.

HABAKKUK 2:3 NKJV

"Dream the impossible dream." Did you know that these lyrics are scriptural? Jesus said it this way, "With men this is impossible, but with God all things are possible" (Matthew 19:26 NIV).

What are your dreams? Perhaps you once had great dreams but your hopes have been dashed, the dreams now lying in the ash heap. Or maybe you're more pragmatic and not willing to set yourself up for possible disappointment.

God has a vivid imagination. And you were created in His image with the ability to dream, because He wants to do great things through you. So no matter what your dreams, God has great dreams for you, and you can throw all of your faith and effort behind them. God specializes in the impossible. Let Him dream His dreams through you.

I can pray the breath prayer, *Let me dream Your dreams, Lord*—

- when my hopes have been dashed.

- to get me out of my rut.

- to fulfill Your design for my life.

- to give me hope.

- to bless others.

- to set my heart on fire for Your purposes.

Let me dream Your dreams, Lord.

YOU ARE MY HIDING PLACE.

You are my hiding place;
you will protect me from trouble
and surround me with songs
of deliverance.

PSALM 32:7 NIV

Did you ever play hide-and-seek as a child?
Ever find that perfect hiding spot that no one ever
discovered? That game is not just for children.
We have an enemy who goes about as a roaring
lion seeking whom he may devour. (See 1 Peter
5:8.) Has he been chasing you lately, his roar
scaring you half to death? Maybe someone is
literally out to get you, or maybe a mountain of
debt is threatening to swallow you whole. Maybe
you are trapped in a dark cave of depression.

The Father has the perfect hiding place for you, one off-limits to the enemy. It is in the shadow of His wings. And not only are you protected there, there is an abundant provision for anything you could possibly need. He blesses you right in front of your enemies, yet they cannot touch you. (See Psalm 23:5.)

Your hiding place is also your home base. In Him, you are secure.

I can pray the breath prayer, *You are my hiding place,* when—

- my enemy is chasing me.

- the storms of life are raging.

- I have nowhere to turn.

- I blow it.

- I'm tired and need to rest.

You are my hiding place.

CARRY ME, LORD.

He tends his flock like a shepherd:
He gathers the lambs in his arms
and carries them close to his heart.

ISAIAH 40:11 NIV

Have you ever seen a toddler hold up their arms to be picked up and carried? When the little one's legs have grown tired from too much walking, no decent parent would ignore the child's plea. At other times, a child might just need some attention and nurturing. If you've ever carried a child, with their head resting on your shoulder, arms and legs wrapped around you, you know what a precious time of bonding it can be.

Children grow up, but that doesn't mean they don't need to be carried from time to time. Can you relate? Your heavenly Father is always

available when your legs have grown tired and
you can't take another step. And He loves it
when you wrap your arms around Him and rest
your weary head on His broad shoulder. It is His
delight to carry you. Climb into His arms today.

I can pray the breath prayer, *Carry me, Lord,*
when—

- I can't take another step.

- I am bruised and bleeding.

- the flood waters are too deep.

- I need to be nurtured.

- my load is too heavy.

Carry me, Lord.

MAY I SPEAK YOUR TRUTH IN LOVE.

When she speaks, her words are wise, and kindness is the rule for everything she says.

PROVERBS 31:26 TLB

Being truthful is certainly a virtue, but it needs to be handled with care. The truth can cut like a knife and do injury to the person on the receiving end. Ephesians 4:15 exhorts us to speak the truth in love. In short, *what* you say matters, but equally important is *how* and *when* you say it! Like the virtuous woman of Proverbs 31, kindness should be the rule for every spoken word. Just as "a spoonful of sugar helps the medicine go down," kindness makes the some-times-difficult truth more easily received.

Doing things God's way—including telling

the truth—is not complicated. No, it doesn't mean that you say every true thought that crosses your mind. It is wise to use discretion. But there's never a need to avoid the truth or tell a lie. God will honor your efforts to speak the truth in love.

I can pray the breath prayer, *May I speak Your truth in love,* when—

- resolving conflict.

- asked my opinion.

- facing rejection or persecution.

- speaking to my children or spouse.

- it would be easier to lie.

- I don't want to.

May I speak Your truth in love.

Increase my hunger for Your Word.

Blessed are they who hunger and thirst for righteousness: For they shall be filled.

Matthew 5:6 nkjv

Ever notice that the more you think about something, the more you want it? Once you start thinking about that piece of hot, oozing-with-cheese, toppings-galore pizza, you just might find yourself calling for takeout.

So why is it so hard to get into the Bible? Number one, you have a very real enemy who does everything in his power to distract you from the powerful words of life that the Bible contains. Number two, people often misread their hunger for God's Word and think they hunger for food, sex, clothes, sports, and any number of other things.

Jesus said, "I am the bread of life. He who comes to Me shall never hunger" (John 6:35 NKJV). There is nothing wrong with food, sex, clothes, or sports as long as they are kept within the bounds set by God's Word; but before you run to the refrigerator, grab your Bible, and enjoy a spiritual snack. Let God fill you up.

I can pray the breath prayer, *Increase my hunger for Your Word*, when—

- I need emotional support.

- I try to satisfy spiritual hunger with other things.

- I wake up in the morning.

- my heart grows cold.

- I become apathetic.

  Increase my hunger for Your Word.

PUT A SONG IN MY HEART.

He has given me a new song to sing,
of praises to our God.

PSALM 40:3 TLB

Isn't it interesting that although it's so hard to remember people's names, a familiar song can stick with you for life? God created music to be a powerful force for good. David literally sang his way out of the doldrums, then left his psalms for us to enjoy. He often poured his heart out to God, but nearly every song ended in victory. Likewise, the apostle Paul sang praises during his captivity in the midnight hour.

It's hard to stay down in the dumps while singing a happy or faith-filled song. They just don't mix. If you're so down that you find it difficult to pray, why not sing instead? When you need a new start, God will give you a new song to pave the way for the miracle He has for you. Even in your darkest hour, God will give you a song of hope. Then when your breakthrough comes, sing a song of thanksgiving.

I can pray the breath prayer, *Put a song in my heart*—

- to encourage me when I'm down.

- as an act of faith that Your victory is coming.

- to soothe my broken heart.

- to praise You.

- as a testimony to others.

Put a song in my heart.

RELEASE ME
FROM GUILT.

*God took away Satan's power to accuse
you of sin, and God openly displayed to the
whole world Christ's triumph at the cross
where your sins were all taken away.*

COLOSSIANS 2:15 TLB

What conversations take place inside your
head? Are they positive and affirming or negative and condemning? Chances are that because
you are acutely aware of your own shortcomings
and failures, not all these conversations are
uplifting. When you're on a guilt trip, the only
two in the conversation are you and the devil.
Not only does he heap on the guilt and shame,
but your guilt indicates that you have been
agreeing with him!

To overcome guilt, you must first recognize that these destructive conversations are taking place. Next, you must kick your accuser out of your thoughts, reminding him of his humiliating defeat at the resurrection. Then invite God and His Word to take up residence, and receive His complete forgiveness. Lastly, you must choose to believe what He says over any other thought that crosses your mind.

Why not talk with your Father right now!

I can pray the breath prayer, *Release me from guilt*—

- and receive forgiveness instead.

- when I remember my past.

- over mistakes I've made as a Christian.

- by helping me forgive myself.

- when others try to condemn me.

Release me from guilt.

GIVE ME WISDOM.

If any of you needs wisdom, you should ask God for it. He is generous and enjoys giving to all people, so he will give you wisdom.

JAMES 1:5 NCV

Life can get tricky. We all do the best we can, but because of our humanness, lapses in judgment are always a possibility. But you don't have to do it alone. Your heavenly Father wants you to succeed in life, and He can help you get there.

King Solomon is considered the wisest man of all time. He was also greater in riches than all other kings, yet he said that wisdom is much better and more profitable than gold! It is fitting that God chose him to record much of his wisdom in the book of Proverbs, and we can partake of it every day.

Of course, God will forgive you and get you back on track when you err; but by filling up on His Word and training your mind to think like He thinks, you have a greater chance of walking in wisdom from the start.

I can pray the breath prayer, *Give me wisdom*—

- regarding the decision I have to make.

- when I'm about to make a mistake.

- on my job.

- in parenting my children.

- when I cannot see the full picture.

Give me wisdom.

I THANK YOU, LORD.

It is *good to give thanks to the* LORD,
And to sing praises to Your name, O Most High.

PSALM 92:1 NKJV

A thankful heart is a happy heart. And we have so much to be thankful for! A heart that beats at just the right pace. The sun coming up every day. Food, clothing, a home. Freedom.

This is not to say that God minimizes your pain when life gets turned upside down or your heart is broken; but He knows that the first step toward healing—the first step out of a dark hole —is to begin giving thanks. By being thankful in the midst of difficulties, you are acknowledging the goodness of God.

The devil does his best to distract us from all

we have to be thankful for by pelting us with negative thoughts. He knows that whatever your mind dwells on will continually get bigger. So short-circuit his plan, and begin giving thanks.

I can pray the breath prayer, *I thank You, Lord,* when—

- I am healthy and happy.

- I'm ill and need to remember all God has done.

- I have a difficult day.

- I forget the God is the greatest blessing in life.

- I need to remember that God will work all things for good.

- I realize just how much I love my family and friends.

I thank you, Lord.

SURROUND ME WITH FAVOR, LORD.

Surely, O LORD, you bless the righteous;
you surround them with your favor
as with a shield.

PSALM 5:12 NIV

Have you ever noticed how VIPs get the royal treatment? Maybe you've experienced this kind of favor on some level. If so, you know what a blessing it is. Or maybe rejection and scorn have plagued your life.

There's good news. You are a VIP in God's eyes! And because you are a child of the King, He wants you to receive the royal treatment. You have complete access to His throne. You don't have to fear His rejection.

God wants you to experience favor with

people as well. He knows the pain of rejection
and has promised to surround you with favor
as a protective shield. That means you can
expect people to treat you fairly and with
respect. Of course, you can't demand this of any
person, but through prayer you can defeat the
enemy who is behind attitudes of disrespect. Use
God's promise of favor as your spiritual sword
to defeat him. God will open doors for you that
no man can shut.

I can pray the breath prayer, *Surround me with
favor, Lord—*

- when others reject me.

- when I need someone's assistance.

- to put me a position to bless others.

- because I'm Your child.

- for promotions.

Grant me favor, Lord.

YOU HAVE DONE GREAT THINGS, GOD.

Our mouths were filled with laughter,
our tongues with songs of joy. . . .
The LORD has done great things for us,
and we are filled with joy.

PSALM 126:2-3 NIV

Oh, the thrill of victory! And the harder the battle, the sweeter triumph is. All of us—including God—love to win, but He *always* wins.

Has God just done the impossible for you? Or are you in the midst of battle, struggling to believe you'll manage to survive, let alone win?

The God you serve specializes in coming out on top, and the more impossible the circumstances, the more glory He receives. Think of the parting of the Red Sea and the greatest victory

64

of all—the resurrection! God told the children of Israel to rehearse His mighty acts over and over. We do well to do the same. Recount the victories He's won for you as well as those in His Word. And as your faith grows, begin claiming the victory for your situation now. He's done it before; He'll do it again!

I can pray the breath prayer, *You have done great things, God,* when—

- I see a sunset or flower!

- I need the faith to believe for an answer to prayer.

- I need help overcoming a bad habit.

- my child needs your help.

- someone comes through for me.

- my prayers are answered.

You have done great things, God.

GIVE ME UNDERSTANDING.

*I pray that your hearts will be
flooded with light so that you can
understand the wonderful future
he has promised to those he called.*

EPHESIANS 1:18 NLT

Are you struggling to understand life and
figure things out? Are you frustrated because
your understanding is limited?

God doesn't want you stumbling around in
the dark, and He urges you not to lean on your
own understanding. Instead you are to seek *His*
understanding, as though it were silver and
hidden treasure. And for good reason! The
understanding found in His Word will enable
you to know the wonderful future God has for
you; cause you to hate every false way (Psalm
119:104); enable you to know God's Word

(Psalm 119:125); help you attain wise counsel
(Proverbs 1:5); keep you safe (Proverbs 2:11);
win you favor (Proverbs 13:15); keep you on the
right path (Proverbs 15:21); be a fountain of life
(Proverbs 16:22); cause you to prosper (Proverbs
19:8); establish your home (Proverbs 24:3); and
make you happy (Proverbs 3:13).

Understanding is a good thing. Pray for it!

I can pray the breath prayer, *Give me understanding*—

- so I can make wise decisions.

- so Your Word will come alive to me.

- to keep me safe.

- to give me a glimpse into the future
  You have for me.

- so I can pass it on to others.

Give me understanding.

YOUR LOVE
NEVER FAILS.

*Love never fails [never fades out or becomes
obsolete or comes to an end].*

1 CORINTHIANS 13:8 AMP

"All good things must come to an end." Not
an encouraging saying, is it? Yet many can testify
that this saying has been their life experience.
On this earth, good things often do come to an
end. People fail. Things happen. Have some
good things in your life failed?

Even though many things in this natural
world will fade away, you have great hope in
God. Think about it: He is infinite. He has always
been and always will be. He is the perpetual I
AM. He will *never* leave you; and since He is
love, and love never fails, His love for you will

never fail—no matter what!

You can count on His love for you. It is an anchor for your soul, it is healing to your heart when it's broken, it lifts you when you are down, it delivers you when you're trapped, it frees you when you are bound, and it comforts you when you hurt. God's love for you *never* fails.

I can pray the breath prayer, *Your love never fails,* even when—

- people reject me.

- I blow it and sin.

- my love falls short.

- I don't love myself.

- the love of people does.

Your love never fails.

MAKE ME BOLD
FOR YOU.

The righteous are as bold as a lion.
PROVERBS 28:1 NIV

Do you consider yourself to be bold and confident, or do you tend to be timid or even fearful at times? Did you know that the Bible says you are as bold as a lion? Yes, *you*—and all who have received Christ.

You can afford to be bold. Jesus triumphed over every foe, and "the one who is in you is greater than the one who is in the world" (1 John 4:4 NIV). God *always* causes you to triumph in Christ. (See 2 Corinthians 2:14.) And if God Almighty is for you, who could possibly be against you? (See Romans 8:31.)

Although you are bold as far as God is concerned, it may take some practice to begin living that way. Start by choosing to believe what God's Word says about you. Begin saying it by faith, "I have been made righteous, therefore I am as bold as a lion." Then begin stepping out to face your fears. Remember, you aren't alone. God is with you, so be bold!

I can pray the breath prayer, *Make me bold for You*—

- in sharing the Gospel.

- when I fear what people think.

- to pray with people.

- to stand up for what is right.

- when I feel like a coward.

Make me bold for You.

REVEAL YOUR PURPOSE.

*I press on toward the goal to win
the prize for which God has called me
heavenward in Christ Jesus.*

PHILIPPIANS 3:14 NIV

What are God's plans for your life? Have you asked Him what they are? Have you asked for a strategy to execute them?

Setting goals helps you get where you want to go in life. Where do you sense God wants you to be in five years? Twenty? At the end of your life? God has a specific plan mapped out for you, and He can help you set goals that He himself will help you reach. Each smaller goal achieved will be one step closer to your overall life purpose.

Every decision you make should be first measured against God's goals for you. If a certain thing will impede your progress, most likely that thing should be set aside. If it will enhance your life and line up with your goals, go for it with gusto.

God created you with a specific purpose in mind. Prayerfully seek Him, and He will begin ordering your steps and unfolding a plan of action. Then, like Paul, at the end of your life you will win the prize for that which God has called you to do.

I can pray the breath prayer, *Reveal Your purpose*—

- for my family.

- at work.

- for my body.

- financially.

- that I might glorify You.

Reveal Your Purpose.

I REST IN YOU.

Do not throw away your confidence;
it will be richly rewarded.

HEBREWS 10:35 NIV

Are you at the end of your rope, struggling to hang on? Are you tempted to just let go and let the chips fall where they may? Well, don't let go just yet—be sure to grab on to God's hand first. Then, let go and let God.

Letting go doesn't mean giving up. It simply means that you quit struggling to make things happen and instead let God do the work. It means refusing to worry and trusting God to fulfill His promises regarding your situation.

The struggle has probably worn you out, but there is rest for you as a child of God. In fact, Hebrews 4:11 NIV exhorts you to "make every effort to enter that rest." It takes practice to let go and let God take over, but the resulting serenity will be worth it.

Don't wear yourself out by trying to do God's part. You do your part by holding on to His promises. Then let go by letting Him do His part.

I can pray the breath prayer, *I rest in You,* when—

- I've grown weary.

- my circumstances are hopeless.

- life is stressful.

- I'm tempted to do things in my own energy.

- I'm tempted to think it all depends on me.

I rest in You.

GIVE ME YOUR WORDS.

*"The Holy Spirit will give
you the right words even as
you are standing there."*

LUKE 12:12 TLB

But I don't know what to say. Have you
ever had that helpless feeling? Maybe someone
you know is gravely ill. You don't know what to
say, so you don't say anything. Or you've felt
that prompting inside to share your faith with
someone, but you held back—again because you
didn't know what to say.

Have you ever taken the promise above and
made it your own? Try doing it now: "The Holy
Spirit will give *me* the right words even as *I* am
standing there." God wants to use you to bless
others, and often that blessing begins with the
words of your mouth. Filling up on God's Word

will place a rich deposit within you. Then, think of it as priming a pump. The next time you get that nudging inside, begin to speak in faith. It's scary at first, but as you begin to talk, the words will flow like rivers of living water.

I can pray the breath prayer, *Give me Your words*—

- so I can encourage others.

- so I can lead others to salvation.

- so I can be Your vessel.

- because they bring life.

- so I can share them with others.

Give me Your words.

REVEAL YOUR PLAN.

"No eye has seen,
no ear has heard,
no mind has conceived
what God has prepared for
those who love him"—
but God has revealed it to us by his Spirit.

1 CORINTHIANS 2:9-10 NIV

Do you know God's plan for your life? Most believers want to walk in God's will, for they know that is where the blessing it. However, many struggle to know what that plan is.

But God says you can know. He will tell you!

"But how will I know? Will He speak to me?" you ask.

Yes, He will—but most likely not in an audible voice. As you immerse yourself in God's Word, the Holy Spirit will enlighten certain verses to you. In prayer, you may get a glimpse of parts of the plan. You may have a prevailing thought that continually grows stronger. He might speak through a friend. Be sure to write these things down because He may use all of these avenues to reveal parts of His plan to you. Expect to hear from Him. One thing is sure, His plans are better than anything you can conceive.

I can pray the breath prayer, *Reveal Your plan*—

- so I can prepare.

- regarding my vocation.

- regarding opportunities to minister to others.

- for my family.

- for my children.

Reveal Your plan.

I AM BLESSED!

*He redeemed us in order that
the blessing given to Abraham might come
to the Gentiles through Christ Jesus.*

GALATIANS 3:14 NIV

"Count your blessings one by one," goes an old Sunday school song. Have you counted yours lately? No doubt you can come up with a list of many things. Recounting them fills your heart with thanksgiving.

Did you know that God wants to bless you even more? Have you read the story of Abraham lately? He was one blessed man. First and foremost, He was God's friend. What greater blessing is there? But there was more. God blessed him with lands, goods, servants, animals, a beautiful wife, his son Isaac, and in countless other ways that few of us can fathom.

Abraham's life was not lacking in difficulties, but the net result was a tremendously blessed life.

None of us has a life free from challenges, but knowing God wants to bless you like He blessed Abraham can be an encouragement to your faith. In those areas of life that seem anything but blessed, begin claiming blessing in that area by faith. It's part of your redemption. You are blessed!

I can pray the breath prayer, *I am blessed*—

- so I can bless others.

- to give You glory.

- on my job.

- even when I have temporary difficulties.

- in my relationships with my spouse and children.

- when I need God's provision.

I am blessed!

YOU ARE THE "LORD WHO HEALS ME."

"If you diligently heed the voice of the LORD your God and do what is right in His sight, give ear to His commandments and keep all His statutes, I will put none of the diseases on you which I have brought on the Egyptians. For I am the LORD who heals you."

EXODUS 15:26 NKJV

Do you think much about the righteousness of Jesus as it applies to your life? That righteousness unlocks many of the promises in the Old Testament, just as Paul said in 2 Corinthians 1:20, "For all the promises of God in Him *are* Yes, and in Him Amen, to the glory of God through us" (NKJV).

God's truth is a powerful thing, and when we attach our faith to it, God can do wondrous things. As in the verse above, one of God's promises to the righteous is to remove sickness from the midst of their family! All of Jesus' righteous life is applied to your account, and He has taken all your guilt upon Himself. This promise is "Yes!" in Christ. God is now, for you, "the Lord who heals you."

When you or your family members are ill, take advantage of the daily blessing of Jesus' righteousness. Worship the Lord and receive His blessing of good health.

I can pray the breath prayer, *You are the "Lord who heals me"—*

- of my allergy symptoms.

- of my flu or some other virus.

- of my chronic condition.

- so I can serve You unhindered.

- so I can be a living testimony of Your healing power.

- so I can triumph over disease.

You are the "Lord who heals me."

MAKE MY HEART LIKE YOURS, JESUS.

*I will give you a new heart
and put a new spirit in you; I will
remove from you your heart of stone
and give you a heart of flesh.*

EZEKIEL 36:26 NIV

What is the condition of your heart? Is it soft and pliable, easily moved with compassion? Weary and burdened? Cold and hard? There's good news if you don't like what you see.

God promises to take away a stony heart and replace it with a heart of flesh. He does this at the new birth when we receive Christ. So, if you are a believer, you already have a heart like that of Jesus!

Unfortunately, the circumstances of life may

have negatively impacted your heart. Stress, sin, and heartbreak certainly affect the condition of one's heart. But Jesus promises rest to the weary, cleansing from sin, and healing for broken hearts. Receive His grace, love, and mercy. Once again, your heart will be like His.

I can pray the breath prayer, *Make my heart like Yours, Jesus,* so—

- I can be an effective ambassador for You.

- I can draw unbelievers to You.

- I will be pleasing in Your sight.

- I will be like Jesus.

- I can be a vessel of Your love, forgiveness, and healing.

- I can bless everyone I meet.

Make my heart like Yours, Jesus.

YOU ARE MY ANSWER.

*In him [Christ] every one of God's
promises is a "Yes." For this
reason it is through him that we say
the "Amen," to the glory of God.*

2 CORINTHIANS 1:20 NRSV

Do you need answers? Your heavenly Father
has them all. When you call upon Him, He will
answer. And if you can find a biblical promise
regarding your situation, His answer is always yes!

When you need wisdom, He promises to
give it. (See James 1:5.) Need healing? By His
stripes, you were healed. (See 1 Peter 2:24.)
Have a financial need? He will meet it according
to His riches in glory. (See Philippians 4:19.)
Your heart hurting? He is your Comforter. (See 2

Corinthians 1:4.) Need advice? He is your counselor. (See Isaiah 9:6.) Need peace of mind? He is the God of peace. (See Isaiah 9:6.) Need hope? He is the God of hope. (See Romans 15:13.) Need love? He is love. (See 1 John 4:8.) Need a friend? He's called you His friend. (See John 15:15.)

He is your answer. And that answer is yes!

I can pray the breath prayer, *You are my answer*, when—

- I am desperate.

- it looks like there's no way out.

- mankind has run out of answers.

- I get confused.

- I don't know which way to turn.

- I can't even put words to my questions.

You are my answer.

GROW YOUR
PATIENCE IN ME.

The fruit of the Spirit is . . . patience.

GALATIANS 5:22 NIV

Ever run short on patience? Maybe you're in
a hurry and your toddler is slowing you down.
Maybe you're trying to meet a deadline and have
to depend on others to get it done. Maybe
you're impatient with yourself, thinking you
should be further along, you should be doing
more, you should . . . (The list can be endless.)

Impatience is nonexistent in God's realm.
He is utterly patient with you because He is
love, and love is patient and kind. It is a fruit of
His Spirit, and He's made it available to you.
Don't expect it to come all at once, however.
Just as fruit takes time to grow and ripen, so it is

with the fruit of patience. But be patient! It will grow as you practice it.

The next time the pressure is mounting, and you're about to blow a gasket; take a deep breath and receive God's patience. It will make you—and everyone around you—happier and more at peace.

I can pray the breath prayer, *Grow Your patience in me* —

- when I'm impatient with myself.

- when I make a mess of things.

- so I can be patient with others.

- when I don't deserve it.

- when my nerves are shot.

Grow Your patience in me.

HELP ME LOOK FORWARD TO THE FUTURE.

*The path of the righteous is
like the light of dawn,
which shines brighter and
brighter until full day.*

PROVERBS 4:18 NRSV

Do you dread the future? Have past circumstances made you cynical? Do world events concern or even scare you? Reading the newspaper or watching the news is enough to depress anyone. Add that to the uncertainties that lie ahead, and a gloomy outlook is not a surprise.

However, none of the above takes God into account. He promises that the future for the believer is good, bright, and full of hope. Life on earth can be scary, but when you abide in the shadow of His wings, He will keep you and your loved ones safe. He's commanded angels to watch over you, and He promises to supply your every need.

Yes, the world is getting darker, but as you abide in Him and His words abide in you, not only will your future be bright, but you will also be a beacon of hope to others.

I can pray the breath prayer, *Help me look forward to the future—*

- and the plans You have for me.

- so I can encourage others.

- so I can reassure my children.

- as I trust in You.

- and let go of the past.

Help me look forward to the future.

91

FILL ME WITH LAUGHTER.

Our mouths were filled with laughter,
our tongues with songs of joy.
Then it was said among the nations,
"The LORD has done great things for them."

PSALM 126:2 NIV

Did you know God likes it when you laugh? In fact, the Bible says that He sits in the heavens and laughs himself!

Sure, life isn't all fun and games, but a little laughter can go a long way toward improving one's outlook and maintaining an overall sense of well being. In fact, Solomon said "a cheerful heart is good medicine" (See Proverbs 17:22 NIV). Another way of putting it—"The joy of the LORD is your strength" (Nehemiah 8:10 KJV).

A heavy and burdened spirit saps your energy, but a joyous spirit enables you to face life with a bounce in your step, a smile on your face, and laughter in your mouth.

As a believer, you have a lot to laugh about. No matter what life throws at you, the end of the Book says that we win! That means we get the last laugh!

I can pray the breath prayer, *Fill me with laughter*—

- because You have defeated my enemy, the devil.

- as You fill my heart with hope.

- because You have blessed me.

- because You work miracles for me.

- so I can inspire others.

Fill me with laughter.

REKINDLE YOUR FLAME IN MY HEART.

He will not break the bruised reed,
nor quench the dimly burning flame.
He will encourage the fainthearted,
those tempted to despair.

ISAIAH 42:3 TLB

Did you know that you are a threat to the kingdom of darkness? The enemy knows that when you are on fire for God, that fire can spread quickly, engulfing everything and everyone near you. It should be no surprise, then, that he sets out to extinguish your flame.

Perhaps you've been beaten down emotionally or even physically. Maybe tragedy has struck your family. The darkness is trying to swallow you up.

But nothing can put out the flame of God's Spirit within you. Know that your heavenly Father sees and knows what you are going through. He wants to encourage your heart and heal your bruises. Take shelter under the shadow of His wings, and allow Him to comfort you and gently blow on your dimly burning flame. It may take some time, but He will stoke the fire until you are burning brightly once again.

I can pray the breath prayer, *Rekindle Your flame in my heart*—

- when it is about to go out.

- when my heart is faint.

- when I'm tempted to despair.

- so I can be a bright witness.

- so I can light the way for others.

Rekindle Your flame in my heart.

MAKE ME YOUR WITNESS.

*You will receive power
when the Holy Spirit comes on you;
and you will be my witnesses.*

ACTS 1:8 NIV

If you find it difficult to tell others about your life with God, you aren't alone. In fact, God must have known it would be a challenge because He sent the Holy Spirit to empower you to be His witness. That doesn't give you permission to bowl people over. A frontal assault rarely bears fruit and can actually do more harm than good. But as an ambassador for Christ, your greatest mission is to take as many people with you to heaven as possible.

Sometimes your manner of living speaks

louder than any words you could say. At other times you need to share your faith verbally. Ask the Holy Spirit to lead you to those who are ready to receive Christ. Staying filled with God's Word and prayer will enable you to share out of the overflow of your heart. Your job is to be sensitive to the Holy Spirit's leading as you step out in faith. Then God will give you the right words to say.

I can pray the breath prayer, *Make me Your witness—*

- to my family.

- to my coworkers.

- so I can take as many people to heaven as possible.

- through my lifestyle.

- with my words.

Make me Your witness.

ALL THINGS ARE POSSIBLE TO YOU, GOD.

*Jesus replied, "What is impossible
with men is possible with God."*

LUKE 18:27 NIV

Does the task before you look insurmount-
able? Has God given you an assignment but you
see no earthly way to accomplish it? Does your
situation seem hopeless?

Well, the God you serve specializes in impossible situations! The Bible is filled with examples
of the miracles God has done for His people.
And since "Jesus Christ is the same yesterday
and today and forever" (Hebrews 13:8 NIV), His
miracle activity is still going on!

One reason He wants you to spend time in

His Word is to build your faith in His ability to do the miraculous in your life. Only God's Word can lift you out of the realm of earthly impossibilities and into God's realm of unlimited possibilities. God knows you can't do it without Him, but as you keep your eyes on Him, you can expect Him to part the waters, slay the giants, and level the mountains before you—whatever it takes to get you to the other side.

I can pray the breath prayer, *All things are possible to You, God,* when—

- I want Your destiny for my life.

- I need to reach my children.

- I need His help on the job.

- I want to renew my love for my spouse.

- I need the impossible.

All things are possible to You, God.

GIVE ME A HEART OF FORGIVENESS.

*"When you stand praying,
if you hold anything against anyone,
forgive him, so that your Father
in heaven may forgive you your sins."*

MARK 11:25 NIV

One of the hallmarks of a Christian is forgiveness—even toward those who are unjust or persecute us. Unlike most other religions of the world, Jesus teaches us to turn the other cheek instead of striking back. Then He says we must go a step further and not only forgive those who wrong us, but bless them!

Forgiveness does not mean that you condone a wrong done to you. It does mean, however, that you set the offender free and commit them to God. Forgiveness is not a feeling. It is a decision—to be like Jesus and to obey His Word. No one said it would be easy, but it is your key to freedom, joy, and an abundant life. The ramifications of bitterness are just not worth it. Let God's love reign in your heart. Be quick to forgive.

I can pray the breath prayer, *Give me a heart of forgiveness*—

- before bitterness can take root.

- just like Yours.

- so I can be free.

- when I am hurt by a friend.

- no matter what wrong is done to me.

Give me a heart of forgiveness.

LET MY WORDS
BE YOURS.

*If you keep your mouth shut,
you will stay out of trouble.*

PROVERBS 21:23 NLT

"Me and my big mouth!" Have you ever
said or thought that? At one time or another,
all of us have said things that would have been
better left unsaid. If you have a quiet or shy
temperament, keeping your mouth shut probably
doesn't pose quite as big a challenge as it does for
a more extroverted person. Either way, the bottom
line is the necessity to think before speaking.

Before you share anything about another
person, ask yourself if you would say the same
thing if that person were there before you.
Will your comment build others up or tear them

down? Is it positive and uplifting or negative and depressing?

Our words have tremendous power. James 3:6 states that "the tongue is a fire" that has the potential to corrupt a person. Choose your words wisely. If in doubt, the thing is probably best left unsaid. Choose your words wisely, and make them a force for good.

I can pray the breath prayer, *Let my words be Yours*—

- when I'd rather strike back.

- to keep me from being snared by my own words.

- instead of my words feeding an argument.

- instead of gossiping.

- when someone confides in me.

Let my words be Yours.

BE MY LIGHT, LORD.

Let us who live in the light think clearly.

1 THESSALONIANS 5:8 NLT

If you were in a mall and the lights went out, there would be a lot of confusion with people trying to get out. People could panic, lose their sense of direction, and possibly get hurt. But if the lights came back on, everyone could regain their bearings and clearly see to get out.

You might never get caught in the dark like that, but mentally this can happen frequently, especially in times of high stress. But stress and confusion are not from God. (See 1 Corinthians 14:33.) In fact, He's given you a sound mind—the mind of Christ. (See 1 Corinthians 2:16 and 2 Timothy 1:7.) And on top of that, the light of the world lives inside you! (See John 8:12.) His Word is a lamp to your feet and a light to your path. (See Psalm 119:105.)

The next time you feel confusion clouding your mind, pull away, and tune in to God's Spirit within you. Let His peace settle your mind. The Light of the World will show you the way.

I can pray the breath prayer, *Be my Light, Lord,* when—

- I have a decision to make.

- I'm in the midst of turmoil.

- confusion tries to overwhelm me.

- I am afraid.

- I'm in the dark.

Be my Light.

MAY I REFLECT YOUR CREATIVITY.

God created people in his own image;
God patterned them after himself.

GENESIS 1:27 NLT

Ever stop to think about how imaginative God is? Everywhere you look there are signs of His awesome creativity. We might be satisfied with one kind of apple, yet He created at least seven varieties of red delicious apples alone! Think of the wide array of plants and animals. The ever-changing sunset. The intricacy of a snowflake.

If you are made in His image—and you are —you have the potential for unlimited creativity! The key is learning to yield to His ideas and being sensitive to His promptings. Keeping your mind filled with His Word and spending time getting to know His voice can lead to increased imagination.

Don't relegate creativity to the arts alone. God wants to give you inventive ways to relate to your children, innovative ideas at work, and ingenious problem-solving skills. You are an original. Let God help you maximize your potential.

I can pray the breath prayer, *May I reflect Your creativity—*

- so Your plans become reality.

- in how I communicate.

- so I can be the best that I can be.

- in relating to my children.

- to keep the spark in my marriage.

- and bring You glory.

May I reflect Your creativity.

HELP ME UNDERSTAND YOUR WORD.

The unfolding of your words gives light;
it gives understanding to the simple.

PSALM 119:130 NIV

Have you ever felt that the Bible is over your head? Some people rely on theologians to interpret it, and don't even bother to try to understand it. But God has given us His Word because it holds the keys to eternal life; a life that begins the moment a person receives Christ.

God knew we might need help, so He gave us the Holy Spirit to enlighten and teach us. The Bible is not like a history book or a novel, because its words are alive and inspired by God. The more you read it, the more insight the Holy Spirit unveils.

Don't make it harder than it has to be. Read the book of John to learn about Jesus. Then try reading the New Testament letters, written by the apostle Paul. They will help you understand your new life in Christ. Ask the Holy Spirit to reveal how the Word applies to you, and He will do it.

I can pray the breath prayer, *Help me understand Your Word*—

- when I am grappling with a problem.

- so that I can apply it to my situation.

- when it seems dry.

- so I can grow as a believer.

- so I can share it with others.

Help me understand Your Word.

109

BREATH PRAYERS FOR WOMEN

SPEAK THROUGH ME, GOD.

*The right word spoken at the right time
is as beautiful as gold apples in a silver bowl.*

PROVERBS 25:11 NCV

Some people have a remarkable way with words. Do you? If not, let the Word of God encourage you.

Jesus said that out of the abundance of the heart, the mouth speaks. (See Matthew 12:34.) Whatever you fill your heart and mind with becomes the reservoir from which your words are drawn. If you are filled with the gloom and doom of the natural world, you won't have anything worthwhile to say at the needed moment. On the flip side, if you feed on God's Word every day, a rich deposit is formed within

110

you. God's words bring life and blessing to the hearer. So instead of fumbling around for the right words, God's Word will begin flowing out of your mouth.

When in doubt, you can always voice words of support and love. They can be the most meaningful words of all.

I can pray the breath prayer, *Speak through me, God*—

- when my friend needs encouragement.

- when my children need some TLC.

- when my sweetheart has had a hard day at work.

- as various people cross my path.

- to help resolve conflict.

Speak through me, God.

GRANT ME FAITH AND COURAGE.

God is our refuge and strength,
A very present help in trouble.
Therefore we will not fear,
Even though the earth be removed,
And though the mountains be carried
into the midst of the sea.

PSALM 46:1-2 NKJV

Did you know that you can refuse to fear? "Yeah, right," you might reply. But it's true. You won't defeat fear overnight, but over time you can develop such confidence in God that fear no longer has power over you.

It is first essential to know God. As with any relationship, the more time you spend with someone, the better you will get to know them.

God's promises reveal what He will do, so as you apply this knowledge to specific circumstances over time, you will develop an unshakeable faith in Him as He brings His words to pass.

When you know God and are confident that He will do what He says He will do, it will be much easier to keep fear at bay; and you will *know* that He will not fail you.

I can pray the breath prayer, *Grant me faith and courage,* when—

- my world gets turned upside down.

- my case looks hopeless.

- fear tries to overtake me.

- the news reports are terrifying.

- I trust You with my whole heart.

Grant me faith and courage.

FILL MY WEAKNESS WITH YOUR POWER.

[The Lord said to Paul], "My grace is sufficient for you, for my power is made perfect in weakness." Therefore I will boast all the more gladly about my weaknesses, so that Christ's power may rest on me.

2 CORINTHIANS 12:9 NIV

Ever feel weak, like you just can't accomplish anything? Thankfully, God didn't leave you here to fend for yourself. He sent the Holy Spirit to fill you with power—the same power that raised Christ from the dead!

By natural standards, the apostle Paul had a very imposing personality. But he knew he was most effective when he was weakest, because it was then that the Holy Spirit could come on the scene and do the miraculous. God received the glory since there was no way Paul could have accomplished the task on his own.

The next time you feel like you "just can't do it," rejoice! Proclaim "Greater is he that is in *me,* than he that is in the world" (1 John 4:4 KJV). As you trust God and take the first step, His power will strengthen you.

I can pray the breath prayer, *Fill my weakness with Your power—*

- so I can overcome addiction.

- so I can overcome depression.

- so I can help others.

- when I am weak.

- so You get the glory.

Fill my weakness with Your power.

LET ME PLAN WITH YOUR WISDOM.

*Any enterprise is built by wise planning,
becomes strong through common sense,
and profits wonderfully
by keeping abreast of the facts.*

PROVERBS 24:3-4 TLB

Lord Chesterfield once wisely stated, "Whatever is worth doing at all, is worth doing well." God wants you to succeed, and you will increase the chances for a favorable outcome if you do several things.

First, make sure the undertaking is God's will. Will it proclaim truth about Him? Does it line up with biblical principles? Once that is settled, look at the enterprise from all angles. Anticipate as many problems as possible. Devise and follow a budget. Make a list of everything you will need. Seek counsel from godly people who have proven themselves through wise planning. Enlist the support of others.

The greatest necessity of all? Prayer. Pray for God's wisdom, His blessing, and His provision. Believe that your steps are ordered of Him. (See Psalm 37:23.) In all your ways acknowledge Him, and He will make your paths straight. (See Proverbs 3:6.) Whether you're establishing a new business, building a home, or raising a teenager, God wants you to plan well, so you can succeed.

I can pray the breath prayer, *Let me plan with Your wisdom*—

- when I undertake a new project.

- in raising my children.

- financially.

- because it will make me more like You.

- regarding my future.

Let me plan with Your wisdom.

HELP ME TO BE GENEROUS.

God loves (He takes pleasure in, prizes above other things, and is unwilling to abandon or to do without) a cheerful (joyous, "prompt to do it") giver [whose heart is in his giving].

2 CORINTHIANS 9:7 AMP

Don't you love to receive gifts? But don't you enjoy it even more when you give to others and see their eyes light up? That's because generosity is a godly trait. God has been so abundantly generous to us, and it is His desire that we turn around and pass the blessing on. Whether it is a gift to a friend, an offering for a missionary, an encouraging word to the downcast, or food for the poor, we are like God when we give.

The Father takes this generosity thing so seriously that He says He is unwilling to do without a cheerful, "prompt to do it" giver. So if you are eager to give, you can expect Him to provide you with the means to bless others. If you want to delight the heart of the Father, be a giver.

I can pray the breath prayer, *Help me to be generous*—

- because I want to be like You.

- because I want to bless others.

- instead of being selfish.

- when it comes to supporting missionaries.

- because it pleases You.

Help me to be generous.

MY HEART YEARNS FOR YOU, GOD.

O God, You are my God;
Early will I seek You;
My soul thirsts for You;
My flesh longs for You
In a dry and thirsty land
Where there is no water.

PSALM 63:1 NKJV

Heart hunger is often misinterpreted as any number of things, such as a craving for food, the drive to succeed, a yearning for intimacy and companionship, or the search for significance. In and of themselves these needs are legitimate, and God promises to meet them. But when you feel a heart hunger for God and think you need food or success, the result is dissatisfaction, loneliness, and emptiness. Only God can fill this longing of the heart.

God created us for fellowship, and since we are created in His image, we likewise have the longing for companionship with Him. It doesn't work to try to fit a square peg into a round hole, so make sure your God-shaped hole gets filled with God—not some inferior substitution. Ask Him to satisfy your heart hunger. He would be delighted to, and your heart will be enriched.

I can pray the breath prayer, *My heart yearns for You, God,* because—

- only You can fill the hole in it.

- You are awesome!

- You make it sing!

- there's no one like You.

- only You can satisfy.

My heart yearns for You, God.

SHINE YOUR FACE ON ME, GOD.

The LORD bless you and keep you;
The LORD make His face shine upon you,
And be gracious to you;
The LORD lift up His countenance upon you,
And give you peace.

NUMBERS 6:24-26 NKJV

You know that great feeling in the spring when there's still some nip in the air, but the sun has begun warming things up? It feels wonderful to close your eyes, look up, and let the sun warm your face.

That's the way God wants you to feel when you look to Him. The world can be a very cold place, but His face shining upon you imparts graciousness and peace. His presence blesses and keeps you. And the great thing is that we don't have to wait for springtime to experience the warmth of His glory.

Regardless of the weather, whether it's a cold, dreary day in winter or a scorcher in August, the Son is shining upon you at all times. Look up and let Him warm your heart today.

I can pray the breath prayer, *Shine Your face on me, God—*

- when I'm feeling blue.

- when darkness tries to overtake me.

- so I can be warmed by Your presence.

- so I can warm others.

- and I'll shine right back.

Shine Your face on me, God.

SHOW THEM YOUR SALVATION.

*[The man] began to tell everyone that
Jesus had healed him, and so he spread the
news about Jesus. As a result, . . .
people came to him [Jesus] from everywhere.*

MARK 1:45 NCV

News travels fast. And that is what happened when Jesus healed this leprous man. Jesus asked the man not to tell others because when people recognized Him, it prevented Him from moving freely from city to city. Yet this man could not contain himself, and he shouted the good news for all to hear. As a result, people sought Jesus out wherever He went.

God has done good things in your life as well. He saved you, for one. What other things has

He done for you? Delivered you from addiction or depression? Healed you of a cold or perhaps a more serious condition? Saved one of your hard-to-reach relatives? Brought your teenager back to Him?

As you testify of God's salvation in your life, also be quick to pray for others. He will make His salvation known to them as well.

I can pray the breath prayer, *Show them Your salvation,* when—

- the media mocks You.

- someone is trapped in sin.

- they forget how much You care.

- that person is lost.

- there is no earthly hope.

Show them Your salvation.

RESTORE TO ME THE JOY OF YOUR SALVATION.

*Restore to me the joy
of your salvation
and grant me a willing spirit,
to sustain me.*

PSALM 51:12 NIV

Remember the exuberance you felt when you first came to know the Lord? In natural terms, it was similar to falling in love. But, like a human love relationship, over time the feelings may have faded. The initial infatuation, the excitement of the wedding, and the passion of the honeymoon may have become nothing more than memories.

But, just as a marriage relationship can be reignited, you can jump-start your relationship with the Lord. By acknowledging that you've fallen into a rut, you've made the first step toward change. Spend some special one-on-one time with Him. Reflect on the exciting times you've shared together. Tell Him of your love. Listen as He reminds you of His unchanging love for you.

Take steps today to rekindle the flame. It will burn brightly once again.

I can pray the breath prayer, *Restore to me the joy of Your salvation*—

- when I miss the closeness You and I once shared.

- because my heart has grown cold.

- when You seem unreal to me.

- as a testimony of Your goodness.

- so I can be a light to the world.

Restore to me the joy of Your salvation.

I PLACE MYSELF IN YOUR HANDS, GOD.

Promotion and power
come from nowhere on earth,
but only from God.
He promotes one and deposes another.

PSALM 75:6-7 TLB

It's a dog-eat-dog world out there. Maybe you've been one of those trampled under the feet of others trying to get to the front of the pack. Unfortunately, it is the way of the world.

But you are not restricted to the world's way of doing things. Whereas according to worldly standards you must work to promote yourself—at all cost, if necessary—it is a matter of trust for the believer. Real promotion comes from God. In the twinkle of an eye, you could go from being a data entry clerk to occupying a place in management. The life of Joseph is a great example of the way God does things, and it can provide tremendous encouragement. (See Genesis 37, 39-41.)

Do your best, be diligent, go the extra mile, bless others. Then trust that the God who created you is capable of promoting you to the destiny He has for you.

I can pray the breath prayer, *I place myself in Your hands, God—*

- because You bless Your children.

- so I will have greater influence for You.

- so my needs will be met.

- when I've been unfairly overlooked.

- according to Your timetable.

I place myself in Your hands, God.

LET ME HEAR
YOUR VOICE.

*"His sheep follow him because they know
his voice. But they will never follow a stranger;
in fact, they will run away from him because
they do not recognize a stranger's voice."*

JOHN 10:4-5 NIV

Have you ever witnessed a baby turn toward
its parents' voice? The baby recognizes both
parents because he or she has heard them since
conception.

Jesus said it would be the same for you.
He is your Shepherd and you are His sheep. You
follow Him because you've heard His voice from
conception, even if you've been unaware of it.
He is speaking all the time—through creation,
through His Word, through His still small voice

inside you. But you must tune your ears to hear Him, just as you would tune in a certain radio station.

Expect God to speak to you; then listen. By reading His Word, you will become more familiar with how He talks and what He says. Then, when a "stranger" tries to steer you off course, you will run the other way because the voice is not the voice you know.

I can pray the breath prayer, *Help me hear Your voice*—

- so I can minister to others.

- through my pastor and godly friends.

- inside my heart.

- through Your Word.

- when I need direction.

Help me hear Your voice.

HEAL MY BROKEN HEART.

*He heals the brokenhearted
and binds up their wounds.*

PSALM 147:3 NIV

There is no pain like that of a broken heart. Have you, like Humpty Dumpty, had a great fall that has left you shattered? You've tried to put yourself back together, but nothing has worked? Perhaps you've tried to numb the pain with shopping, food, work, or drugs. Those things can only mask the brokenness. They are incapable of healing and can never make you whole.

Jesus understands a broken heart. Imagine the depth of His pain when those He loves reject Him. He knows what you are going through, He cares, and He is here to heal you.

All the king's men couldn't put Humpty back together, but you have the King of Kings to restore you. And not only will He heal your heart and bind up your wounds, He will set you back on the path to fulfill your destiny. He will also lead you to others whose hearts have been broken so you can pass on His healing touch.

I can pray the breath prayer, *Heal my broken heart*—

- when the man I love has rejected me.

- when my parents have hurt me.

- when a friend has abandoned me.

- when I feel like a failure.

- so I can pass on Your healing.

- because only You can provide real healing.

   Heal my broken heart.

SURROUND ME WITH YOUR PRESENCE.

*You have made known to
me the path of life;
you will fill me with joy
in your presence,
with eternal pleasures at
your right hand.*

PSALM 16:11 NIV

Have you ever sensed the presence of God? It is very real and in many instances tangible. Of course you shouldn't base your Christian walk on feelings, but God does want you to experience the joy of His presence—a joy that surpasses any earthly joy or thrill.

Begin by spending some time alone with Him. Then lift your voice in praise. You could read a psalm out loud to get started. It might help to sing along with a worship CD. As you praise Him, you will sense the peace of His presence. Joy will begin to well up within you as you get a glimpse of His glory and awesomeness.

You can bask in God's presence anytime, anywhere. You are a carrier of His very life.

I can pray the breath prayer, *Surround me with Your presence*—

- as I go about my daily tasks.

- when I'm having a rough day.

- when I'm encouraging a friend.

- during my commute to and from work.

- so I can delight myself in You.

Surround me with Your presence.

FREE ME FROM
MY PAST.

As far as the east is from the west,
so far has he removed
our transgressions from us.

PSALM 103:12 NIV

Did you know that your past does not define who you are? You may have made horrendous mistakes, been abused or neglected, but that is not who you are. God doesn't even have knowledge of the transgression once you've asked Him to forgive you!

Only God can heal pain resulting from your past, but He will. Partake of His abundant forgiveness. Bask in His healing grace. Let Him into the dark and ravaged areas of your soul. He will make you whole.

You will most likely never forget the problem in your past, but God will take away the sting of it. He will help you make peace with it. When your own mind or other people begin to condemn you, you will be able to toss the matter aside because the issue has been settled.

I can pray the breath prayer, *Free me from my past*—

- so I can get on with life.

- and free me from torment.

- because You don't remember it.

- when others remind me of it.

- when I think about it.

Free me from my past.

I TRUST YOU TO SUPPLY MY NEED, GOD.

*My God shall supply all
your need according to His riches
in glory by Christ Jesus.*

PHILIPPIANS 4:19 NKJV

What need are you facing? Is it financial? Is your marriage in trouble? Is your job on the line? Do your kids need a father? Do you need peace of mind?

No matter what you need, your heavenly Father has the provision and is eager to give it. Notice that the verse doesn't say He will meet your need according to your checkbook or how wealthy your relatives are. His provision doesn't depend on where you live or who you know. No, God dispenses his provision according to

His riches in glory by Christ Jesus. Jesus Christ accomplished all that was necessary to meet your every need when He hung on the cross.

Your Father doesn't want you to go without —in any area. When you are in need, it is difficult to have anything to give others. God is an abundant provider. He promises to provide enough for your needs, but also a surplus so that you can be a blessing to others.

I can pray the breath prayer, *I trust You to supply my need*—

- for contentment.

- for companionship.

- for forgiveness.

- according to Your glorious riches.

- so I can help meet the needs of others.

   I trust You to supply my need.

BE MY FATHER.

*"Do not be afraid, little flock,
for your Father has been pleased
to give you the kingdom."*

LUKE 12:32 NIV

What do you think of when you hear the word *father*? Does it make you feel warm inside, nurtured, and cherished? Or do you feel put down, abused, fearful? Abandoned? Numb? Unfortunately, many earthly fathers are not what their children need them to be. Has this been the case for you?

Jesus wants to make sure you have an accurate picture of the Father. Jesus described Him as being eager to give you His very kingdom. Jesus even indicated that the Father loves *you* as much as the Father loves Him! (See John 17:23.)

It may take some time and effort on your

part, but if you will reflect on the Father's wonderful attributes revealed in His Word, a new image will be formed. Your earthly father has had a profound impact on you. Whether that impact has been good or bad, your heavenly Father will exceed your expectations.

I can pray the breath prayer, *Be my Father*—

- when I need to be nurtured.

- when I need provision.

- to replace the negative image I have had.

- when I need to be surrounded by Your big, strong arms.

- and the One who delights in me.

Be my Father.

MAY I LIVE IN THE NOW.

"Do not worry about tomorrow, for tomorrow will worry about itself. Each day has enough trouble of its own."

MATTHEW 6:34 NIV

Living in the present is harder than it sounds. It seems that human nature wants to either dwell on the past or concentrate on the future. What's the case with you?

Dwelling on the past likely means you're stewing over something you can't change or resting on yesterday's laurels instead of conquering new vistas today. Dwelling on the future indicates you are fretting over things that might never happen or you are living for tomorrow—you'll be happy *then*. Either way, you're missing out.

We can certainly enjoy fond memories of the past and learn from past mistakes. And we should plan for the future. But to get stuck in either place will cheat you of the blessings right in front of you.

Once today is over, you can never go back. Give today your all, and take advantage of every blessing God intends for you to experience today.

I can pray the breath prayer, *May I live in the now,* when—

- I worry about the future.

- my past haunts me.

- I'm afraid of tomorrow.

- I'd rather yearn for the "glory days" of yesterday.

- I'm cheating myself out of today.

May I live in the now.

HELP ME OVERCOME EVIL WITH GOOD.

*"If your enemy is hungry, feed him;
if he is thirsty, give him something to drink.
In doing this, you will heap burning
coals on his head."*

ROMANS 12:20 NIV

When someone hurts you, you want "to get 'em and get 'em good," don't you? You want to give the person a taste of their own medicine.

But what would Jesus do? That is the question for the believer. Although the pain or injustice may be very real, the believer is to respond with love—not threats, shouts, or revenge.

Strife takes you out of the realm of God's blessing and makes you susceptible to darkness.

Love, on the other hand, overlooks an

144

offense. The best way to "get back at" your
enemy is to bless them. They won't know how
to handle it. It's the goodness of the Lord that
leads to repentance. (See Romans 2:4.) Your act
of kindness may be just the thing to win that
person to Christ.

Love never fails.

I can pray the breath prayer, *Help me overcome
evil with good*—

- when someone cuts me off in traffic.

- so I reflect Your love for the offender.

- when I'm treated unfairly.

- when everything in me wants to blow up.

- because love never fails.

Help me overcome evil with good.

FIND ME, GOD.

*I myself will tend my sheep and have
them lie down, declares the Sovereign LORD.
I will search for the lost and bring
back the strays. I will bind up the injured
and strengthen the weak.*

EZEKIEL 34:15-16 NIV

Did you ever get lost as a child? One minute
you might have been walking beside one of
your parents, the next you found yourself
separated from him or her—lost! Being lost can
be terrifying. You can lose your bearings and
become confused. Is this where you are today?
Lost, scared, confused?

You are never lost as far as God is concerned.
When you call upon Him, He hears you and
He will answer. He knows right where you are,
even if you don't have a clue, and He knows

how to bring you back to safety. He will clean and dress your injuries and fill you with His strength. Then, when you are ready, He will put you on the right path so you can safely resume your journey.

I can pray the breath prayer, *Find me, God,* and—

- when I call on You, You will answer.

- I trust You to show me the way.

- You are with me.

- You will never leave me.

- in You, I am found.

Find me, God.

I GIVE YOU THANKS, GOD.

*You turned my wailing into dancing;
you removed my sackcloth and
clothed me with joy,
that my heart may sing to you
and not be silent. O LORD my God,
I will give you thanks forever.*

PSALM 30:11-12 NIV

Voicing thanks accomplishes several things. First, it conveys appreciation and respect for the giver. This is why *Thank you* is one of the first phrases parents teach their children.

Thanksgiving can also lift your spirits. Giving God thanks for all that He has done in your life helps you focus on all of your many blessings instead of the things you *don't* have. It helps you realize that your life isn't so bad after all.

Expressing your thanks can also be an expression of faith. If you are asking God to supply a certain need, you can thank Him before you ever see the answer, because you know He will fulfill His promises regarding the matter.

Finally, it's just more enjoyable to be around those who are thankful. Give God thanks forever!

I can pray the breath prayer, *I give You thanks, God,* for—

- getting me out of that jam.

- my family and friends.

- saving me.

- answering my prayer.

- forgiving me when I fail You.

- loving me so much.

I give You thanks, God!

I REST IN YOUR PEACE.

*My [own] peace I now give and
bequeath to you. Not as the world gives. . . .
Do not let your hearts be troubled,
neither let them be afraid.
[Stop allowing yourselves to be agitated
and disturbed; and do not permit
yourselves to be fearful and intimidated
and cowardly and unsettled.]*

JOHN 14:27 AMP

Do you tend to be a worrier? You wonder,
"What if . . .?" Given the state of the world, it's
understandable.

But did you know you can stop allowing
worry to agitate and disturb you? Of course you
can't pull that off in your own strength, but
because Jesus left you *His* peace—which is far
superior to any earthly peace—you can flush out

every trace of anxiety. When you develop confidence that God will deliver you no matter what you face, fears about the future suddenly lose their power. He will prepare a table before you in the very presence of your enemies. (See Psalm 23:5.) He always causes you to triumph in Christ! (See 2 Corinthians 2:14.)

I can pray the breath prayer, *I rest in Your peace,* when—

- worry affects my enjoyment of life.

- stressful events happen.

- those I love encounter problems.

- finances look grim.

- I need to remember that You will be there for me.

I rest in Your peace.

I SEEK YOUR FACE, LORD.

God is at work within you,
helping you want to obey him, and then
helping you do what he wants.

PHILIPPIANS 2:13 TLB

Do you ever feel guilty because you know you should pray, but you don't? If so, you are in good company. In the Garden of Gethsemane, Jesus asked the disciples to pray with Him. Unfortunately, the men's hearts were willing, but their flesh was weak.

You have an advantage over the disciples, however. When you received Christ, God came to live *in* You, to work in you, and to help you obey!

Setting aside times for prayer will help you

BREATH PRAYERS FOR WOMEN

develop intimacy with God, but prayer is not relegated to any set time, place, or method. Prayer is simply talking to God. You can do that in the shower, in the car, while you walk on the treadmill, while you do housework. You can even pray under your breath in a crowd of people.

God will increase your desire to pray and then help you do it.

I can pray the breath prayer, *I seek Your face, Lord—*

- when nothing is going on.

- because I want to please You.

- for the needs of others.

- out of respect for You.

- so I can know You better.

I seek Your face, Lord.

MAY I REFLECT YOUR GENTLENESS.

Your gentleness has made me great.

PSALM 18:35 TLB

It is common for gentleness to be equated with weakness, but nothing could be further from the truth. In fact, many earthly principles run crosswise to God's way of doing things. Many who are first on earth shall be last in heaven, and the last first. (See Mark 10:31.) Even if we feel weak, with God we are strong. (See 2 Corinthians 12:9.) You get the idea.

Gentle people are confident people. They know they don't have to overpower others in order to reach or motivate them. They understand that a spoonful of sugar helps the medicine go down.

You can afford to be gentle because God has

been gentle to you. Instead of zapping you in your sinful state, He reached down and saved you, gently tucking you under the shadow of His wings. Then He placed the fruit of gentleness in you to grow and mature. As you yield to that fruit instead of giving place to harshness, the fruit of gentleness will ripen so that others may partake of God's nature through you.

Want to be great in the kingdom of God? Be gentle.

I can pray the breath prayer, *May I reflect Your gentleness—*

- to bring healing to others.

- because You are gentle.

- when I am angry.

- instead of harsh.

- with the weak and hurting.

May I reflect Your gentleness.

CAUSE MY FAITH TO GROW.

*We ought always to thank God for you,
brothers, and rightly so, because
your faith is growing more and more.*

2 THESSALONIANS 1:3 NIV

Seeing is believing. Or is it? Remember Doubting Thomas? The disciple who had to touch Jesus after the crucifixion before he'd believe it was really the Master? It's easy to relate to Thomas—it's human nature.

But you aren't just a human anymore. You are a new creature in Christ Jesus! When you received Christ, you also received "the measure of faith" (Romans 12:3 NIV). All Christians start out with faith, and it can grow just like any living thing grows. Faith enables you to look

beyond what you see with your physical eyes to
the
reality of what God says in His Word.

As you hear and meditate on God's Word,
your faith in His presence, goodness, and power
will begin to grow. And as you apply your faith
to situations in your life, even more growth
and confidence will take place as God fulfills
His promises.

I can pray the breath prayer, *Cause my faith to
grow—*

- when I worry.

- when I need Your help.

- as I hear Your Word.

- when something is bigger than
  I can handle.

- so my prayers will be effective.

Cause my faith to grow.

I BLESS YOU, LORD.

I will bless the LORD at all times;
His praise shall continually be in my mouth.

PSALM 34:1 NKJV

Heaven is an awesome place; and one day, you will get to go there if you have received Christ. Imagine worshiping God with all the saints around the Father's throne. Imagine the glory, the splendor, the exhilaration of singing His praises and blessing His holy name.

Actually, you can get a foretaste of that glory right here on earth, every time you open your mouth to bless the Lord. Everywhere you look there is something to praise the Father for—the glory of a sunset, the first flowers of spring, a hug from a child. The list is endless